Anger Management

Developing The Practice Of Emotional Regulation,
Serenity, And Proficient Temperament Handling

*(Methods That Are Proven To Be Successful In Managing
Your Emotions)*

Ruben Crawford

TABLE OF CONTENT

A Comprehensive Comprehension Of Anger 1

Strategies For Managing Anger Through Self-Help Techniques 6

A Deeper Dive Into The Various Forms Of Anger 15

Discover The Triggers 28

Breathing Therapy 45

Understand The Factors That Elicit Anger And Common Misconceptions Surrounding Anger 52

Is Rage A Frequent Issue? 82

Check Your Belief System 95

Expectations From Birth To The Third Year 125

Acquire Awareness Of Your Triggers And Employ Efficient Strategies For Their Management 147

A Comprehensive Comprehension Of Anger

What is anger? How can one determine if they are experiencing anger? Is it regarded as inappropriate for my child to experience feelings of anger? These queries hold significant importance and may currently be occupying your thoughts. Anger is a universally experienced emotion, serving as an inherent reactionary mechanism triggered by feelings of endangerment or vulnerability.

It may be characterized as an innate emotional reaction to a perceived danger, engendering a inclination to confront or dismantle the presumed origin. Numerous expressions can be employed to convey feelings of anger. Examples of such vocabulary consist of rage, madness, and fury.

Ultimately, it indicates an underlying issue. Anger serves as an indicator that either you or your child is experiencing physical or emotional harm inflicted by someone or something. This demonstrates that anger constitutes a vital emotion necessary for our sustenance.

Nevertheless, anger does have adverse consequences. Anger can give rise to detrimental consequences such as the manifestation of aggression, hostility, and violent behavior. The sentiment can be associated with numerous fractured relationships, health ailments, subpar performance, and challenges with figures of authority. In the pages of this literary work, I aim to direct my focus towards the issue of anger pertaining to the younger generation.

In accordance with the research conducted by Lewis &Michalson, anger can be delineated into three fundamental components:

1. The emotional condition of anger; this corresponds to the affective or activation state; the sensation that emerges when a desired outcome is impeded or a requirement is obstructed. Among the challenges children may face in their daily lives are:

Disputes relating to personal belongings: these can emerge due to persistent pestering or intimidation by a peer attempting to encroach upon their territory.

Physical aggression: encompasses the act of forcefully exerting pressure or inflicting harm upon an individual by another child, extending to the extent of physical confrontation. It could also potentially originate from you as a parent or a disgruntled educator.

Verbal altercation: this could be a persistent source of provocation or mockery regarding something she may or may not have done. As previously mentioned, it can originate from both individuals within one's age group as well as from individuals who are older.

Exclusion: your child may experience social isolation or be denied the opportunity to engage in play with their peers.

Concerns regarding adherence: this entails requesting your child to engage in activities against their personal preferences.

2. Manifestation of frustration; there are numerous methods through which your child may display his or her anger. He or she may opt to sulk, shed tears, or communicate it through their facial demeanor. They may adopt more

assertive measures to protect themselves.

These techniques could involve either physical or verbal reprisals directed towards the individual they perceive as causing harm. The individual may choose to steer clear of the entire situation, or endeavor to evade it.

3. A comprehension of anger: the capacity to regulate this sentiment is directly associated with comprehending it. The capacity of your child to engage in introspection regarding their anger is confined, necessitating your or the teacher's intervention in order to provide guidance.

Let us enhance our comprehension of anger manifestation in children.

Strategies For Managing Anger Through Self-Help Techniques

You have identified your predicament, made a resolute determination to resolve it without hesitation, and initiated the initial measure. It is imperative to grasp, at the outset of this arduous undertaking, that despite its challenging nature, progress can only be made through a methodical approach, one step at a time. The resolution of your anger issues will require more than just a single effort, and the alleviation of frustration cannot be achieved through a one-time application of the suggested strategies. It constitutes an iterative procedure, necessitating your discernment and determination of the most optimal approach for your circumstances. Nevertheless, awaiting you at the culmination is an individual of tranquility, equanimity, and emotional resilience - a persona that has perpetually been your aspiration. Moreover, the expedition is truly not as protracted as it may seem!

The initial stage of the process involves cognitively recognizing and acknowledging your anger. Engaging in the act of evasion, suppressing your emotions, and attributing your frustration to an extraneous factor will yield no positive outcomes. Anger should not be immediately perceived as negative, but rather acknowledged in order to address it effectively. Nevertheless, it is important to distinguish between recognizing the existence of anger and engaging in inappropriate displays of it. Once you acknowledge the presence of aforementioned entity, it is imperative to adopt a methodical and organized approach in order to articulate it.

Immediate Calming Techniques

To effectively eliminate sentiments of anger and hostility, it is imperative to examine their underlying roots and address them directly. Nevertheless, this is a gradual and ongoing process that leads to improvement over an extended period. In the interim, it is imperative for you to familiarize yourself with effective methodologies that can be employed to promptly alleviate anger when it arises. Based on your chosen means of communication, you have the opportunity to determine the most effective approach for yourself and strive towards achieving emotional and behavioral equilibrium in that specific instance. Speculation comes later.

In the majority of individuals, intense anger is typified by the impulse to vociferate, engage in physical aggression, or experience profound bodily unease and exasperation. In light of the aforementioned, irrespective of the underlying factors, there exist a multitude of calming methodologies at your disposal.

Retrain your brain

As previously outlined, anger is an acquired behavioral pattern. Your emotional response is due to the fact that you have conditioned yourself to react with anger to specific stimuli. The sole means to address this issue is through the process of retraining one's brain to elicit a different response.

You have the opportunity to engage in this activity on a daily basis using the subsequent methods:

● Behave towards others with the same respect and consideration that you would expect to receive. In the event of an individual committing an error, it is advisable to refrain from promptly reacting with anger. Take a moment to ponder and contemplate how you would prefer to be treated in the event that you committed a comparable error.

● Prior to speaking, consider the potential impact of your words by placing yourself in the recipient's position and contemplating how such a statement might make you feel. Is it respectful? Is it kind? Would it result in an improvement or a deterioration of the situation?

● Exercise mindfulness regarding your physical sensations. Is your heart racing?

Is your face flushed? Is your respiration rapid or labored? In the event that an affirmative response is provided to any of these inquiries, it may be advisable to allocate a brief period for introspection or engage in the practice of a mindful respiratory exercise. It is crucial to maintain composure in all circumstances, particularly when faced with tense or volatile situations.

Presented below are several effective techniques for effectively managing and regulating the emotion of anger:

● Firstly, it is imperative to acknowledge the prevailing issue.

● Secondly, maintain a meticulously documented journal where you record every instance that triggers your anger. It will be necessary for you to document the sequence of events, the underlying cause of those events, and the manner in which you responded to them. It is imperative to acquire the skill of recognizing personal triggers and acknowledging instances where one may have exhibited an exaggerated reaction. This journal will facilitate a deeper self-understanding while enabling you to proactively identify your triggers prior to their activation.

● Lastly, it is imperative to establish a robust framework of support. Take into account the possibility of imparting the knowledge of your pursuit in acquiring anger management skills to your significant other, immediate family members, or your closest confidants. Kindly request their vigilance in observing your behavior, assisting in the identification of triggers, and providing support in attaining tranquility during episodes of anger. In addition to providing motivation, support, and facilitating your learning, expressing acknowledgement of your challenges will enhance the bond you share with them.

● Additionally, in instances where one's emotions become overpowering, and a sense of anger emerges, it is advisable to employ a method known as an "interruption technique." The primary purpose of such techniques is to effectively disrupt one's immediate response, allowing for a moment of reflection and the subsequent re-establishment of self-control. Interruption techniques include:

Engaging in a controlled breathing technique.

⏺ Counting to twenty.

Engaging in a ten-minute meditation session.

◌ Engaging in a brief stroll within the vicinity of the local community.

Engaging in therapeutic writing to document and reflect upon sources of distress.

Engaging in attentive auditory reception of your preferred musical composition.

Recalling and reflecting upon the positive aspects within your life.

A Deeper Dive Into The Various Forms Of Anger

The prevalence of anger among adults in our nation is increasingly becoming a significant concern. As we progress into the future and witness a growing relinquishment of our capacity to manage circumstances, it increasingly challenges our ability to stay abreast of the developments surrounding us. This can potentially elicit frustration among a sizable number of individuals due to the relinquishment of control, heightened stress levels, and the additional burden of responsibilities.

Having acknowledged that, it should be noted that there exists a diverse array of anger manifestations, all of which are subject to situational influences and are apt to be exhibited in varying manners.

We have observed a range of twelve prevailing manifestations of anger among adult individuals, comprising:

Intense rage—individuals who exhibit this type of anger often exhibit a propensity for swift loss of control and a direct confrontation with the perceived source of their anger. Frequently, this refers to another individual, although it may also denote an animal or an inanimate object. Trouble making, physical harm, and defiance could be examples of this kind of anger.

Individuals manifesting chronic anger often exhibit an enduring displeasure towards themselves or their circumstances, devoid of any discernible provocation or underlying factor, encompassing a general discontentment with their lives and, at times, a profound dissatisfaction with their surroundings or the global environment. These individuals appear to constantly display a perpetually irate disposition.

Positive frustration - these individuals channel their feelings of anger towards actions that result in benefits for others. They might channel their anger and dedicate their efforts towards a noble cause in response to their distress.

Intentional anger—when an individual seeks to establish dominion over individuals, circumstances, or objects, they manifest indications of this anger. A significant number of individuals afflicted with such anger harbor a strong desire for power, and this yearning persists even in the absence of victory.

Evaluative resentment—a tendency of this individual to vent their anger through critical remarks or public degradation of others. They are essentially employing their anger as a means of asserting their superiority.

Intense rage may manifest in individuals who perceive their circumstances as confining or unfavorable. They will inflict harm upon others or themselves, whether through physical or verbal means, in an attempt to extricate themselves from the given predicament.

Paranoia-infused rage emerges when an individual harbors an inherent dislike for others, irrespective of any actions or behaviors exhibited by those individuals. Frequently, it is due to a combination of fear and jealousy that this behavior is brought to the surface.

The individual exhibits a tendency towards dormant anger, wherein the anger is not overtly expressed and may not be addressed openly. On occasion, they will articulate their perspective in a manner that portrays themselves as the aggrieved party. They might employ the use of sarcasm or employ offensive language.

Reciprocal anger, often observed among males, refers to the prevailing form of anger triggered as a response to the anger of others, without any additional provocation.

Self-directed anger—this phenomenon poses a significant danger as the individual is prone to causing harm to themselves as a consequence. The frustration will be internalized instead of being addressed through constructive means.

Verbal anger denotes the expression of anger through spoken language, wherein the individual may employ derogatory or hostile remarks towards the source of their anger.

A manifestation of intense anger can frequently be observed in the form of verbal or physical aggression. It is a transient variety that exhibits variable manifestations ranging from mild to severe bouts of anger.

It is apparent that a diverse range of anger manifestations among adults can occur at different instances, exhibiting considerable variation among them. Acquiring the skills to identify these indicators and effectively reduce their occurrence is the most ideal approach to ensure the preservation of one's physical and emotional well-being, thereby preventing anger from exerting a dominant influence on one's life.

Self-compassion Facilitates Behavioral Transformations

Upon my initial encounter with the concept of self-compassion, I perceived it as an indulgent and impractical endeavor incompatible with the demands of reality. Nevertheless, I encountered several noteworthy research studies that altered my perspective. These studies have demonstrated the correlation between self-criticism and the development of reduced self-esteem, heightened anxiety, and depressive symptoms.

Each of these three factors has the potential to exacerbate your anger; however, it is fortunate that self-compassion can mitigate these influences.

Instead of engendering complacency, self-compassion amplifies one's drive to effectuate positive lifestyle modifications, notwithstanding any obstacles encountered. Consequently, the cultivation of self-compassion will empower individuals to persist in their anger management program, even when confronted with a disheartening setback.

Self-compassion is associated with diminished levels of stress and anxiety, heightened emotional well-being, and improved adaptation to significant life transitions. Given that self-compassion effectively mitigates stress and anxiety, it facilitates enhanced regulation of one's temper.

Self-compassion facilitates personal growth, enabling one to manifest their most authentic and optimal self. It grants individuals the ability to cultivate self-acceptance whilst simultaneously endeavoring to rectify those aspects of their conduct that necessitate amelioration.

-Del Hickson

Upon further reflection, I have come to the realization that when my friends and family are excessively critical of themselves, it is compassion that I extend to them. What are the reasons for exhibiting compassion towards my loved ones while neglecting to extend the same level of care and consideration towards myself?

In cultivating self-compassion, one is inclined to acknowledge their inherent imperfections, recognizing them as shared traits among the vast global population of approximately seven and a half billion individuals. By bestowing upon oneself compassion, one acknowledges the fallibility inherent in every individual. Each individual faces challenges, commits errors, and occasionally experiences setbacks.

Upon recognizing that I was not the sole individual grappling with episodes of irate reactions, I started experiencing diminished feelings of seclusion. I can leverage my recently developed self-compassion as a constructive catalyst to sustain my commitment towards improving my anger management program. On each occasion that I experienced a recurrence of anger, the practice of self-compassion empowered me to alleviate my self-deprecating cognitions, permitting me to promptly regain my composure and resume my intended course of action.

Similar to those individuals who grapple with unregulated anger, I possessed a tendency to engage in rumination whenever I experienced a loss of temper. Rumination refers to the process of incessantly replaying a distressing event or personal setback within one's thoughts. Additionally, it may encompass engaging in constant self-criticism regarding one's shortcomings or lack of success.

In addition to causing negative emotions, rumination can induce a state of emotional disempowerment. In the current state of mind, your inclination towards undertaking constructive steps to ameliorate your circumstances is diminished. Luckily, self-compassion serves as a formidable mechanism to thwart the progression of rumination and discouragement.

You have been engaging in self-criticism for an extended period of time with limited effectiveness. Attempt to embrace self-acknowledgment and observe the outcome.

-Louise L. Hay

Self-compassion Reduces Self-criticism

The individual with whom you allocate the greatest amount of time is none other than yourself. If an individual consistently engages in self-critical behaviors, they may frequently encounter feelings of frustration and irritation towards themselves. This consistent and recurrent irritation at a non-significant level poses challenges in managing one's anger.

Excessive self-criticism can impede anger management as it tends to influence one's behavior towards others in a similar manner as it influences how they perceive themselves. On the other hand, as one develops self-compassion, they also cultivate an increased sense of compassion towards others. This instigates self-regulation of one's emotional responses by fostering a harmonious equilibrium between exasperation triggered by an individual's bothersome conduct and understanding and compassion towards their circumstances.

Dr. Kristin Neff undertook a perceptive and rigorous research study, which was subsequently published in the esteemed Journal of Research in Personality. The research revealed that individuals who practice self-compassion encounter reduced levels of anxiety in times of stress. Due to their diminished levels of anxiety, individuals are inclined to think with enhanced clarity, thereby increasing their propensity to refrain from exhibiting fits of anger.

Discover The Triggers

Having familiarized yourself with the prevailing forms of anger, we may now progress to the examination of factors that incite or provoke anger, commonly referred to as anger triggers. Each individual possesses unique characteristics, yet as you peruse this compilation, it is possible that you may identify with one or several of the prevalent stimuli based on your personal experiences.

To ascertain the presence of anger issues, it is crucial to examine not only behavioral patterns but also the associated emotional and physical symptoms. We will review the catalysts within the contents of this chapter.

Anger Triggers

The occasional encounter with minor feelings of displeasure does not indicate a requirement for anger management. Occasional ire is a universal experience that should be acknowledged, as long as it is channeled in constructive manners, anger can yield positive outcomes. When confronted with persistent anger and thoughts that evoke intense rage, it becomes necessary to examine one's behavioral patterns to ascertain the underlying causes of pain and distress.

Should you live a highly demanding and accelerated lifestyle, it is conceivable that you remain unaware of the precise catalysts that incite your anger. During the upcoming week, it is imperative to duly observe and assess your conduct to identify any emerging issues. Pose inquiries to yourself using the following set of prompts to discern if any resonate with you.

1. Do I harbor sentiments of mourning or sorrow? Have I experienced the recent loss of a cherished individual or the culmination of a significant, enduring relationship?

The experience of sorrow and melancholy may elicit intense emotions of resentment if adequate time for recovery from the circumstances has not been granted.

2. Am I experiencing a sense of being overwhelmed with my workload? Am I assuming a larger workload than I am realistically able to manage? Does

my commute prove to be excessively challenging and result in significant exhaustion upon my arrival home?

A demanding occupation can significantly contribute to feelings of anger, particularly when one experiences a sense of powerlessness and lacks the means to address their role or workload.

3. Do friends and family members perceive me as being easily taken advantage of? Do I perceive that individuals underestimate my value and interact with me in a manner that indicates a disregard for my opinions?

If individuals do not perceive you with due seriousness or if you experience unease in expressing refusal, it is plausible that sentiments of resentment may arise, potentially culminating in the emergence of anger.

4. Did I experience a sense of disappointment or betrayal? Have I been deceived or betrayed by an intimate partner, acquaintance, or relative? Has my trust been violated by any individual?

The revelation of an individual's act of infidelity, dishonesty, or theft can be profoundly distressing. If one discovers themselves dismissing their injured emotions, it is plausible that anger might be intensifying covertly and escaping notice.

5. Is financial hardship a challenge I am currently facing? Does one encounter difficulties in meeting their rent/mortgage obligations and covering other recurring monthly expenses? Is it the case that I am

incapable of ensuring a satisfactory standard of living for my family?

Experiencing financial difficulties can generate feelings of inadequacy, and the inability to meet the fundamental needs of oneself and one's family is a significantly justifiable cause for frustration.

6. Am I sexually frustrated? Is it possible that I am experiencing repressed sexual desires and perceiving a lack of outlets to express my sexual emotions?

Sexual tension represents a genuine phenomenon, and in the absence of proper self-expression or physical release, it can potentially manifest as anger or frustration.

7. Have I been misusing substances? Could the medications I am currently

taking potentially be causing alterations to my cognitive functions?

The utilization of illicit substances and certain prescribed drugs can greatly contribute to the manifestation of anger issues. When under the influence of substances, there is a notable alteration in cognitive function, which can also be observed with certain pharmaceutical interventions.

8. Have I incurred an injury that has resulted in a disability or rendered me incapable of engaging in certain activities that I greatly enjoy? Do I have a grave medical condition?

Given the significant nature of this inquiry, it has the potential to unlock the root causes of your anger-related challenges. If you currently find yourself in a circumstance where your life has undergone significant transformation due to either physical injury or illness, it is possible that you might experience feelings of anger whose underlying cause may remain unclear. It is perfectly acceptable to experience such emotions, and it is equally vital to express them. You will experience rapid improvement.

What findings did you acquire during your examination of the trigger list? Did any of the inquiries evoke profound emotions? Occasionally, it is the circumstances that elicit the greatest unease, which necessitate our direct confrontation. Thoroughly review the questions prior to proceeding to the subsequent section of the book. One might encounter unexpected revelations upon contemplation of the inquiries for an extended duration. I have observed that residual emotional wounds that I believed I had already overcome were the underlying cause of my current state of anger. Examine the events and experiences from the previous five years, as well as your formative years, for the resolutions you seek. This occasion calls for genuine introspection.

ANGER

We will commence by precisely delineating the concept of anger. What is anger? Anger represents an emotional condition that encompasses a spectrum of intensities, ranging from subtle irritations to overwhelming fury and rage. Similar to various emotions, anger is accompanied by psychological and physiological alterations. Specifically, when experiencing anger, there are noticeable increases in heart rate, blood pressure, as well as elevated levels of energy hormones such as adrenaline and noradrenaline. Rage is an inherent and beneficial sentiment. Even when disproportionate to its trigger, experiencing anger on a frequent and intense basis can have detrimental effects on both interpersonal relationships and an individual's psychological well-being and overall quality of life. Repressing and accumulating anger may also have detrimental and enduring consequences.

ANGER MANAGEMENT

The management of anger encompasses a diverse set of competencies that aid in the identification of anger indicators and the effective management of triggers in a constructive manner. It is imperative for an individual to recognize the presence of anger at an initial stage and proceed to articulate their needs with composure and self-assurance. The concept of anger management differs from suppressing one's anger. The control of anger is a proficiency that, akin to any other proficiency, can be acquired through consistent effort, dedicated practice, and, undoubtedly, a considerable amount of patience. If the intensity of your anger is exerting an adverse impact on your relationship, particularly when it escalates into acts of violence or poses other forms of peril, it is advisable to seek guidance from a mental health expert or consider enrolling in an anger management program.

WHY MANAGE ANGER?

Anger exhibits a spectrum of intensity, spanning from slight vexation to fervent fury. Although a significant portion, perhaps around 80% of the populace, classifies anger as a "negative emotion," it can also possess positive qualities. Indignant emotions can motivate individuals to advocate for others or instigate transformative shifts within society. It is possible that it bears resemblance to the examples I have previously cited.

Nevertheless, unaddressed feelings of anger can potentially result in the manifestation of aggressive conduct, including vocal outbursts directed at others or acts of property damage. It may potentially induce individuals to isolate themselves from society, foster significant antisocial tendencies, directing their anger inward, thereby detrimentally affecting their overall health and well-being.

Anger can have detrimental effects on one's physical, mental, and social well-being when it is frequently or intensely expressed. This is the reason why it is imperative to implement anger management techniques in order to identify constructive methods of expressing one's emotions.

What is the underlying cause of my propensity for readily experiencing anger?

There are numerous factors that could lead to one feeling anger. Possible other way to say this in a formal tone: "It may manifest as manifestations of fear, panic, stress, financial challenges, relationship difficulties, or traumatic experiences." As previously indicated, mood disorders have the potential to incite feelings of anger, as well as induce hormonal discrepancies.

CONTROLLING ANGER

The charity "Mind," which is a prominent organization focused on mental health in the United Kingdom, outlines three primary measures for effectively managing anger.

- Identify the initial indicators of anger.

- Allow yourself ample time and room for processing the stimuli.

- Implement strategies that can aid in managing anger

RECOGNIZING YOUR ANGER

Controlling anger in the heat of the moment can present a considerable challenge. Nonetheless, early detection of the emotion can prove to be crucial. It enables an individual to channel their cognitive attention towards a more advantageous perspective. Anger elicits the release of adrenaline, which is the hormone associated with the 'fight-or-flight' response, priming an individual for potential confrontation or peril. This may lead to diverse consequences such as increased heart rate, accelerated respiration, general muscular tension, agitation, pacing, clenched fists and jaw (particularly prevalent), perspiration, and tremors. These physiological reactions may indicate an appropriate reaction to a given circumstance. Detecting the indication in a timely manner enables an individual to evaluate whether the stimuli justifies such a physiological reaction.

STEP BACK

The acquisition of additional time can prove essential in mitigating an enraged reaction. This can encompass straightforward measures. When faced with a triggering situation, it may be beneficial to engage in a brief period of counting up to the number ten, engage in a brief stroll, or establish communication with an individual who is not directly involved, such as a trusted friend, family member, or professional counselor. In this manner, you have the opportunity to articulate your emotions verbally. Additionally, it can prove beneficial in mitigating the situation while potentially discerning the root cause of the heightened emotions.

Breathing Therapy

One of the initial observations that can be made when experiencing an elevation in both the level and strength of fury is the tendency for one's respiration to become rapid and shallow. An essential aspect of anger management involves instructing individuals on how to regulate their breathing effectively, thereby aiding in the abatement of anger. These deep breathing exercises can serve as a transient diversion. It encompasses more than mere diversion; in fact, it entails the inversion of the innate physiological reaction of the body to feelings of anger. Engaging in regulated respiration during episodes of anger communicates a message to the body, facilitating the initiation of a calming process following the discharge of adrenaline throughout the system. Additionally, it aids in the restoration of a harmonious equilibrium of carbon dioxide and oxygen within the body, counteracting the imbalanced levels prevalent during states of tension.

Initially, acquiring the ability to regulate your breath may pose certain challenges. Acquiring proficiency in controlling one's breath during moments of anger necessitates a considerable investment of time, exertion, and unwavering commitment. There exist individuals who relinquish their efforts after merely attempting breathing control techniques for a solitary week and subsequently proclaim to others that the method is ineffective. However, this perception arises due to their inadequate allocation of time for the technique to manifest its intended effects, as well as their potential lack of genuine commitment to its practice from the outset. It might be advisable to engage in regular practice of these breathing techniques, even in circumstances when you are not experiencing anger. By adopting this approach, you contribute to the facilitation of your respiratory exercises when confronted with a distressing or infuriating circumstance. Additionally, it will facilitate the establishment of a benchmark for self-regulation of emotions.

When commencing a respiratory exercise, it is beneficial to engage in it within an ideal setting that fosters personal comfort, such as one's own bed. If, however, you find yourself incapable of seeking alternative options, it is acceptable under the circumstances. The majority of these respiratory exercises can be performed in any location. When engaged in the process of regulating your respiration amidst a circumstance characterized by escalated levels of anger, it is imperative to initially ascertain the point at which your breathing begins to adopt shallow and irregular patterns. After performing the aforementioned action, the subsequent course of action is to cease. Cease and assess the current state of affairs.

Why Anger?

Various emotions elicit a range of distinct sensations. As an illustration, the experience of happiness can elicit a smile and induce a sense of pleasantness. Conversely, anger elicits heightened cardiovascular activity, induces perspiration in the palms, and engenders a general sense of discomfort. Indubitably, anger elicits an unpleasant sensation, wouldn't you agree? Rage has the potential to elicit feelings of fear or even anxiety. From an early age, societal norms have ingrained in us the belief in the pursuit of pleasure. It essentially signifies that we have been predisposed to pursue diverse positive emotions while disregarding any undesirable or distressing experiences. If one experiences a sensation that induces discomfort, it is likely that one will seek to eliminate it by any means possible. This profound inclination to suppress your anger or unleash it in a fit of rage is detrimental to your well-being.

Have you ever pondered the potential benefits of experiencing emotional discomfort?

Many individuals find anger to be a discomforting emotion. It gives rise to physiological responses characterized by considerable distress, elicited by an individual's feelings of anger. Furthermore, it can be highly unpleasant when one becomes the target of the ire of others. Occasionally, individuals have a tendency to presume that others harbor resentment towards them, despite the absence of any substantiating evidence. One's rage can be profoundly intimidating. To illustrate, the emotional distress that arises from your parental resentment not only engenders feelings of guilt, but it also disrupts your emotional equilibrium. Due to anger's inherent discomfort, the task of examining one's emotions or comprehending the underlying catalysts of one's anger is compounded. Additionally, it becomes challenging to comprehend your anger. Nevertheless, anger constitutes a fundamental emotion, serving a crucial role that cannot be disregarded.

It is imperative that you comprehend the fact that anger will give rise to a sense of discomfort. This precisely demonstrates how anger directs attention towards words themselves, and such attention should not be disregarded. Each and every emotion that you encounter, including anger, possesses crucial significance and performs a significant role in your existence. In order to gain a genuine understanding of your emotions, it is imperative to cultivate the ability to embrace and endure certain forms of discomfort. Please be advised that progress and transformation are unattainable without experiencing some level of discomfort. Presented herein are a few justifications for the potential benefits of embracing anger.

Understand The Factors That Elicit Anger And Common Misconceptions Surrounding Anger

Familiarize yourself with indicators and catalysts of your anger.

The emotion of anger activates the physiological "fight or flight" response within your body. Even in instances where one experiences intermittent outbursts without prior notice, there are discernible physiological indicators that signify the body's inclination to respond with anger. Recognizing and comprehending these indicators will enable you to implement measures to effectively regulate your anger prior to it becoming unmanageable.

Take note of the bodily sensations associated with anger: Are your muscles experiencing tension, are your hands or jaw tightly clenched, is your stomach experiencing a sensation of tightness? Are you experiencing an elevated heart rate or an accelerated breathing pattern? Do you experience any symptoms of facial redness or excessive perspiration?

Recognize and analyze your cognitive patterns: Recognize the negative patterns in your thinking that frequently lead to the emergence of anger. One might perceive that anger is being triggered by external factors such as events, situations, or individuals causing frustration. Nevertheless, anger issues frequently stem from cognitive patterns characterized by pessimism. As an instance, one might possess a steadfast perspective regarding the ideal course events ought to take, leading to feelings of annoyance and fury when confronted with a divergence from said expectations. Alternatively, perhaps you attribute the negative occurrences in your life to external sources instead of assuming personal accountability for your circumstances.

Identify circumstances that elicit anger: It is important to note that stressful situations should not be used as justification for anger. However, gaining awareness of the impact these events and situations have on you can assist in avoiding unnecessary provocation. Do you experience frustration as a consequence of the recurring delays caused by everyday traffic? Alternatively, do you engage in altercations whilst queuing at the doctor's office or within the confines of a grocery store?

Myths About Anger

First Myth: The inheritance of anger. Frequently, individuals hold the misconception that the propensity for exhibiting extreme anger is predetermined through genetic inheritance, and thus, unalterable. Nevertheless, the empirical evidence from scientific research indicates that individuals do not possess innate anger-related predispositions. Conversely, these studies indicate that the manifestation of anger is socially acquired, and individuals can effectively regulate their anger through the implementation of anger management strategies.

Fallacy 2: The manifestation of anger invariably leads to acts of aggression. There exists a prevailing misconception that the sole means by which anger can be diminished is through the utilization of aggressive forms of expression. Please be advised that it is essential to consider alternative approaches for conveying anger that are productive and assertive.

Successful anger management entails a range of techniques and strategies.

Misperception 3: A necessity for achieving one's desires is to display assertiveness. Frequently, individuals tend to improperly conflate assertiveness with aggression. The objective of aggression is to instill fear, exert control, cause harm, or inflict injury upon another individual, reflecting a mindset that prioritizes victory regardless of the consequences. Conversely, the objective of assertiveness is to convey sentiments of displeasure in a manner that is considerate and courteous towards others. Communicating in a confident manner entails refraining from imposing threats or blame onto others, thereby decreasing the likelihood of causing emotional harm.

Myth 4: Expressing anger is consistently advantageous. In opposition to prevailing beliefs, the forceful manifestation of anger through actions like striking pillows or screaming is not conducive to overall health and therapeutic well-being. Research indicates that individuals who choose to express their anger aggressively tend to enhance their capacity for anger expression. To put it succinctly, expressing anger in a hostile manner serves only to reinforce aggressive conduct.

Three: Varied Expressions of Anger

As mentioned in preceding sections, each individual among us frequently encounters feelings of anger. We each possess individual variations with regard to the frequency at which we experience anger, the level of intensity associated with our anger, and the subsequent actions that stem from our anger.

With reference to these three parameters, we are able to categorize anger into the subsequent levels:

Irritation

This represents the initial stage of anger. It is activated when we perceive something unfavorable within our surroundings. It is customary for us to recognize the origin of our vexation, yet we typically relinquish this sentiment promptly upon being diverted by external stimuli. In a state of irritation, our responses to the cause of our dissatisfaction are restrained. We simply allow them to coexist without disruption and continue with our daily endeavors.

Certain individuals are capable of maintaining this level of anger consistently throughout the entire year. It is a common observation that we all know an individual who possesses an unwavering sense of positivity and cheerfulness, to the extent that they remain impervious to anger, regardless of the circumstances.

Anger

This represents the second tier. Prolonging irritation can potentially give rise to feelings of anger. In contrast to annoyance, individuals who experience anger are more inclined to outwardly express their emotions. An instance that illustrates this phenomenon occurs when an individual publicly reprimands someone for the act of queue-jumping. A significant portion of the population encounters episodes of anger on a biweekly basis.

This type of anger may serve a specific intention. It can serve as a catalyst for motivating an individual to take action against what they perceive as unjust. This anger is within a reasonable and appropriate range for emotional expression. Individuals who possess the ability to contain their anger within a secondary threshold are those who invariably exhibit a purpose or objective in the manifestation of their anger. Additionally, they refrain from allowing their emotions to dictate their speech, vocal intensity, and behavior.

Rage

The third tier comprises of boundless wrath. This stage is distinguished by a succession of adverse behaviors prompted by anger. Rather than merely singling out an individual, an individual who is consumed by anger may vociferate with an intimidating demeanor. In the event of a challenge, he might resort to physical altercation with that individual.

Other individuals may demonstrate anger through persistent and relentless verbal mistreatment directed at their intended recipient. In contrast to the preceding stage, anger lacks a defined purpose or objective. Individuals who frequently encounter feelings of intense anger frequently find themselves precipitating the deterioration of interpersonal bonds and tarnishing their reputation within the community.

Intense fury has the capacity to induce a state of temporary unconsciousness, leading individuals to engage in actions they would not typically consider or condone. Certain individuals who have been convicted of criminal offenses have admitted to experiencing temporary episodes of unconsciousness due to extreme emotional states, such as profound anger, during the commission of their unlawful actions. This phenomenon is commonly identified as an instance of "uncontrolled anger".

Upon completion of this literary work, your objective will be to avert succumbing to fury when confronted with anger in the future. It is not possible for each one of us to maintain a consistently positive demeanor at all times. Nonetheless, each of us possesses the ability to regulate our responses to anger, thereby averting the escalation into a rage-induced episode.

4

The dissimilarities between Anger and Hostility

Upon initial observation, it may appear that they share similarities in theory and principle, however, their actual nature differs dramatically. According to its definition, anger can be described as an intense form of displeasure directed towards a specific thing or individual. According to its inherent definition, anger is a natural emotional response commonly observed in human beings, typically considered as a constructive expression of emotions.

However, the significance lies in how individuals choose to channel their anger. The matter that spurred anger may only elicit minimal emotional response in individuals, prompting them to casually mention it to their neighbor in passing. Alternatively, it may upset an individual to the extent that they embark upon establishing an organization to formally address the issue.

Both the virtuous and the wicked are susceptible to the effects of anger...The inadequate handling of one's anger frequently emerges as the foremost challenge we encounter within society. The three most straightforward methods to identify ineffective management of anger are as follows;

When an individual remains angry for an excessive duration

When the magnitude of anger greatly surpasses the significance of the matter (overreacting).

When an individual suppresses their anger until it reaches a critical point where they physically erupt or begin to encounter adverse health ramifications.

Antagonism exemplifies the disintegration of harmony, an overarching aversion towards ideas and principles, and a comprehensive adversarial attitude towards life. Hostility is broader in scope as an attitude or even as a way of existence. We can conceptually define hostility as a fundamental underlying lack of trust towards society and its constituents.

In a general sense, individuals with a cynical demeanor often exhibit an overly dramatic reaction to circumstances (engaging in overreaction).

The response... one might contemplate these are matters that I do appear to possess and would not solely desire the diagnoses but also a method to transform and evolve into a less combative individual. The response to that inquiry is somewhat redundant yet remarkably straightforward.

It is known as affirmation and I will explain the process. Provided below is a set of 'esteem building questions'. Prior to addressing potentially stressful issues or individuals, I recommend posing these questions to yourself.

3 – Acquiring the Skills of Social Interaction

Engaging in constructive exchanges with others consistently leads to an enhanced sense of well-being. By employing the exercises presented in this chapter, you will observe a reduction in your stress levels and an improvement in your self-perception. A significant portion of our emotional experiences greatly influences our perception of ourselves. For instance, individuals with diminished self-worth do not abruptly awaken one morning harboring intense self-disdain. Their sentiments arise from the constant repetition of messages that instill in them a sense of worthlessness.

"You are useless"

You have failed to meet my expectations.

"You are lazy"

The manner in which you progress is influenced by the entirety of adverse criticism received in your life, and this also holds true for the emotion of anger. If an individual provokes your anger and you have experienced difficulties in managing and suppressing this emotional reaction, the anger persists and engenders a transformation in your character, rendering you markedly pessimistic. You must mitigate this by carefully selecting the individuals with whom you associate. While such behavior is not acceptable within a professional setting, you will discover that surrounding yourself with encouraging and amicable individuals contributes significantly to your personal well-being, ultimately diminishing the likelihood of yielding to anger.

A good deed

Although it may sound cliché, daily endeavors to positively impact someone's life can significantly enhance one's inner happiness. Make a conscious effort each day to consider actions that could bring about increased happiness in the lives of others. It is not necessary for it to be anything out of the ordinary. This can encompass actions such as volunteering to transport a neighbor'schildren to school, warmly welcoming individuals with a cheerful demeanor, reaching out to a friend whom you have not been in contact with for some time, or even bringing a cake to your workplace for collective enjoyment. One could also consider performing a kind gesture such as preparing a cake to gift to an elderly resident within the immediate vicinity. You are incorporating a facet of affirmative engagement into your life. When confronted with anger, the state of equilibrium in the various aspects of your life will prevent your mind from instinctively succumbing to a state of anger. You exhibit a propensity for exercising increased prudence when it comes to expressing anger, likely due to your awareness of its detrimental impact upon others. Doing a good deed every day puts you in the frame of mind that is giving. Those individuals who are often inclined to give are typically characterized by their ability to let go of anger, and this exercise primarily aims to cultivate such a disposition.

4:

Strategies for Managing Individuals Exhibiting Anger in Your Surroundings

Frequently, we find ourselves in the midst of individuals exhibiting discontentment, often without our conscious awareness. Wherever one may travel, there is invariably someone who harbors discontentment either towards a specific action that may have been committed against them, or towards unrelated matters that do not align with their preferences.

There exist specific physiological indications that individuals may exhibit when experiencing anger. They may exhibit indicators of discomfort such as bruxism, hand tension, averted gaze, or physical avoidance. Additionally, one shall observe alterations in their facial characteristics, characterized by a reddening of the complexion and the protrusion of veins. They might exhibit accelerated respiration or even voluntarily cease breathing to manifest a cyanotic discoloration. Their lips may experience dryness, cracking, or even bleeding as a result of persistent biting. A alteration in their voice shall also ensue; it grows in volume, strength, and rasp. Their disposition may likewise undergo alterations, as they tend to exhibit a withdrawn demeanor and diminished approachability. When these manifestations become apparent, it can be inferred that an individual is experiencing anger.

When faced with the presence of individuals of this nature, how do you typically respond? It is advisable to refrain from engaging in any form of collaboration with them. If it is feasible for you to relocate to an alternative area within the room or perhaps a separate room altogether, please consider doing so. If such a circumstance proves infeasible, endeavor to minimize verbal interaction with them. Kindly refrain from inquiring as responses may be provided with a heightened, irritable disposition or demeanor. Express regret and persist without giving significance to their presence to the greatest extent feasible. Please acknowledge their presence in the event of any interaction, but refrain from engaging in any further conversation.

Please find below a comprehensive guide on proficiently handling individuals who are experiencing anger in your vicinity.

#1. Refrain from instigating conflict with them and instead work towards defusing the situation until they regain their composure. [Aristotle]

On occasion, despite the perception of committing a significant error, it is imperative to remain firm in one's decision to pursue what is morally correct. Hence, it is advisable not to yield in the face of irrational individuals, irrespective of whether they direct their anger towards you.

By taking this action, you will effectively impart to them the correct methods for resolving their issues, thereby establishing yourself as a role model for them. It is not within one's prerogative to compel individuals to change their ways, but it is plausible that they may emulate those who possess unique qualities and characteristics.

#2. Exercise caution in engaging with potentially vengeful individuals harboring resentment towards others, so as to prevent or mitigate conflicts and their ramifications on personal and global scales. [Seneca]

It is imperative that you refrain from associating with individuals who believe they are entitled to everything, regardless of their conduct. Individuals experiencing anger management issues often face numerous challenges and tend to struggle with maintaining a rational perspective on the world.

While it might be tempting to engage with individuals who are angry, it is advisable to refrain from doing so and prevent them from imposing their skewed perception of existence. It is advisable to assume that they will consistently remain opposed to you, regardless of the circumstances.

3. Attentively listen and comprehend their desires, exhibiting restraint in refraining from speaking until their emotions have subsided. [Marcus Aurelius]

Marcus Aurelius provides superb yet unambiguous counsel on how to handle individuals who exhibit unreasonable anger. There is an undeniable difficulty in refraining from responding to individuals who are discontent, with the aim of seeking their departure. However, it is undeniably more beneficial to proactively avoid engaging in conflicts.

Should you desire to attentively hear their input, it is advisable to initially refrain from interrupting them and instead engage in a seated interaction that promotes effective expression on their part.

1: Developing the Capacity for Forgiveness

The process of acquiring the ability to manage one's anger commences with cultivating self-compassion, and subsequently broadening that sense of compassion towards others. Demonstrating self-compassion is frequently a more challenging task in actual practice than it is in theory.

The majority of encyclopedias and dictionaries tend to describe forgiveness in a general manner, specifically as a transformative procedure involving the release of negative emotions or the cessation of animosity or resentment towards others. This definition lacks a crucial component, specifically, the inclusion of other emotions such as anxiety, shame, grief, and guilt. These also constitute fundamental elements of anger.

When endeavoring to practice forgiveness and effectively let go of one's anger, it is imperative to carefully examine the manner in which one's mind may be inclined to retain feelings of resentment and the underlying motivations behind this inclination. Do you hold a subconscious belief that your anger serves as a means of ensuring your safety? Does anger serve as a shield for concealing something? If that is the case, may I inquire as to which aspect of your being you are endeavoring to shield from harm? What purpose does anger serve within the context of your life?

On numerous occasions, we find ourselves confronted with circumstances wherein we desire to relinquish our resentment towards a particular matter, yet we encounter significant difficulty in doing so. What is the strategy to overcome such an impediment? In what manner can one effectively manifest their intellectual yearning for forgiveness?

Similar to any other matter, it can be beneficial to approach forgiveness as a sequential progression.

A considerable number of individuals perceive it as beneficial to grant themselves the authorization to undergo the process of forgiveness assimilation at a personal, individualized pace. When considering the matters of forgiveness and grief, the sole timetable that should be followed is that which aligns with one's individual circumstances. The process will naturally unfold for you, and it is inadvisable to exert undue pressure on yourself to engage in forgiveness at a pace that exceeds your readiness. Acquiring forgiveness often necessitates a significant period, occasionally spanning across several years.

It could potentially be beneficial in substantiating your emotional experience of anger. Although it may seem peculiar, there are occasions when anger can be considered a justifiable reaction. As an illustration, there was a woman I had acquaintance with, whose son had met an unfortunate demise due to an intoxicated motorist. For an extended period, she harbored intense animosity towards the driver of the truck responsible for the tragic loss of her child, a reaction that is well within the bounds of human nature. She was accurate in perceiving that she had been deprived of her possessions and unjustly separated from her child. Her belief that the driver should not have operated the vehicle while under the influence was accurate. Her anger was justified, legitimate, and conducive to her well-being.

Is Rage A Frequent Issue?

On a daily basis, individuals across the globe encounter circumstances or challenges that may incite anger within them. This sentiment has been ingrained within the fabric of every individual's being, serving as a fundamental tool for the preservation of life. Conversely, at the opposite end of the spectrum, uncontrolled anger can result in fatality for individuals unable to effectively cope with it. How? Research has indicated that anger can lead to improbable hazards, including cardiac conditions, heart attacks, and severe occupational harm.

Although anger is a universally experienced emotion, certain individuals possess the tendency to develop it as a recurring personal characteristic, thereby making it challenging for them to effectively regulate. It resembles the scenario of an individual struggling with alcoholism, expressing a desire to abstain from consuming alcohol, but ultimately engaging in excessive drinking. An ingrained behavior, whether positive or negative, can seamlessly integrate itself into an individual's daily routine to the point where it is performed unconsciously. It has become an ingrained aspect of their daily routines.

So is anger. Anger has the potential to develop into a recurring characteristic that can exert a negative influence on interpersonal dynamics, encompassing the detrimental impact it can have on one's overall well-being. Stepping outside your comfort zone to proactively address anger management may pose challenges; however, it is an attainable endeavor.

Presented below are several misconceptions surrounding anger, intended to provide clarification on its prevalence or rarity:

- Men are more prone to anger compared to women. When considering the incidence of anger, there is no distinction to be made between males and females. The disparity can be attributed to the varying levels of emotional intensity pertaining to the experience of anger. Research has indicated that males tend to exhibit a proclivity towards experiencing heightened levels of anger. Contrarily, it is observed that women tend to harbor their anger for extended periods of time.

- Experiencing anger is undesirable. A strategy employed by individuals to manage stressors is to experience anger. Experiencing anger may serve as a defense mechanism against feelings of vulnerability and apprehension, providing a surge of heightened vitality, enhancing one's self-assurance, and facilitating improved interpersonal communication. The world underwent a significant transformation towards being more livable with the emergence of individuals like Martin Luther King Jr. and Gandhi, who fervently expressed discontent with prevailing circumstances.

- It is beneficial to experience anger. Expressing anger can result in favorable outcomes, although not in circumstances involving self-mutilation, substance dependence, domestic violence, gastric ulcers, sexual misconduct, or property destruction.

• The frank articulation of your anger gives rise to an issue. • The overt manifestation of your anger exacerbates the situation. • The unreserved display of your anger transforms it into a matter of concern. • The explicit communication of your anger renders it problematic. Merely about 10% of individuals possess the knowledge and willingness to openly articulate their sentiments of anger. The remaining individuals, constituting 90% of the population, have a tendency to conceal, refute, or suppress their feelings of anger. Individuals who repress their anger are the ones who must learn to effectively manage their emotions, while those who express their anger tend to receive more attention and can initiate action.

- One's disposition tends to become more irritable with advancing age. • The level of irritability typically increases as one progresses in age. • As one grows older, a tendency towards increased crankiness becomes apparent. Contrary to popular belief, elderly individuals generally exhibit lower levels of anxiety compared to their younger counterparts.

Examining the Financial Implications of Anger

Anger possesses dual facets. Anger can provide advantages and access to various resources. These are the beneficial outcomes of experiencing anger, although it is important to acknowledge that there are also associated drawbacks and costs to expressing anger. An important aspect regarding the costs associated with anger is that they can lead to either favorable or unfavorable outcomes, with the underlying responsibility resting solely on us as individuals. The evaluation of anger's cost is contingent upon our methods of expression and interactions with others. Once you have successfully mastered the art of regulating your anger, you will inevitably surpass the boundaries of your own expectations and accomplish greatness. Nevertheless, should one allow their anger to surpass a reasonable threshold, the outcome will be an overwhelming rage characterized by violent tendencies. Your demeanor exhibits tendencies of violence and aggression towards anything that displeases you, demonstrating an unwillingness to tolerate outcomes that are not aligned with your expectations. It is commendable to exhibit concern regarding the financial implications of one's anger. The term "cost," as employed in this context, encompasses both the advantageous and disadvantageous consequences stemming from anger. Gaining awareness of these expenses will facilitate your self-evaluation, as well as enable you to scrutinize your familial and professional aspects, discerning the origin of the difficulties you are encountering.

THE BENEFIT OF ANGER

In our contemporary society, it is commonplace for individuals to perceive anger as a detrimental sentiment that necessitates effective management in order to foster prosperous interpersonal relationships and professional encounters. It is inadvisable to engage in public discourse regarding your instances of anger. It would be more appropriate to maintain silence and project an air of composure and serenity in the presence of others. Nevertheless, in light of the prevailing fallacy that anger is an inherently negative emotion, it is pertinent to acknowledge that anger possesses distinct merits and virtues. You may not wish to persist in harboring extensive obliviousness regarding the subject of anger. Over the years, certain indicators of anger have consistently demonstrated reliability. By comprehending this fact, you will enhance the quality of your life, interpersonal connections, and professional endeavors. Numerous individuals encounter difficulties in the present day and on occasion, when in solitude, they ponder, "Why did I behave in such a manner last night? Perhaps I should have exhibited more empathy and attentive listening towards him; perchance then he would not have experienced distress." Frequently, when confronted with challenges, it seems probable that our tendency to become angry has contributed significantly to the negative outcomes before us. Indeed, it is possible that we could encounter such difficulties as a result of our anger. Nevertheless, on certain occasions, the issues we encounter might not originate from lingering anger. You may find it intriguing to learn that your anger can occasionally contribute to the alleviation of your challenges. The tangible consequences resulting from the anger you experienced might have been significantly mitigated through the outward manifestation of your anger. Occasionally, in instances where anger is being utilized in a constructive manner, it may appear as though it is producing an adverse outcome. In the long term, one eventually perceives the positive impact of harboring anger. In instance where your anger leads to positive outcomes, it is conceivable that you may not be present to acknowledge the fruition of these results, instead, focusing solely on the negative aspects. In order to comprehend the constructive nature of anger, it is imperative to engage in the process of cognitive restructuring and direct your attention towards suitable objectives. When anger is communicated with moderate intensity, it typically yields constructive and gratifying outcomes.

The societal, cultural, and religious constituents experienced by countless individuals have presented challenges when endeavoring to perceive the favorable aspects and practicality of anger. This ideology, in certain circles, has redirected the focus from the righteous expression of anger to the aggressive and combative manifestation of heightened anger. Consequently, a prevailing belief among many individuals is that one stands to benefit from refraining from succumbing to bouts of anger. You have likely been informed about the detrimental nature of your anger and its potential to impede your progress towards attaining certain goals. While there is some validity in all of these perspectives, it is crucial to acknowledge our deficiency in effectively discerning between the two manifestations of anger in certain contexts.

Science, psychology, and other mental health professionals have played a pivotal role in addressing the shortcomings inherent in our culture and various belief systems. Their contributions primarily revolve around identifying the beneficial effects that anger can yield when properly channeled. I have discerned ten principles or advantages associated with anger. Subsequently, I shall enumerate them and provide concise explanations.

Check Your Belief System

You become aware that a friend has referred to you in a derogatory manner. How would you respond and formulate your thoughts in light of this situation?

Your thoughts would promptly inquire as to the reason behind his remark, thereby initiating a cascade of reflections that would lead you to recall various prior occurrences where he has exhibited unkind behavior towards you and others. Your thoughts will become inundated until you arrive at the conclusion that his level of malevolence surpasses your own. On your next encounter with this friend, you may find yourself experiencing a sudden surge of anger, leading you to contest and disrupt each of their utterances.

The primary obstacle concerning beliefs arises from their gradual formation within us, necessitating a steadfast and resolute commitment on our part to effect any change. Whenever you encounter information that contradicts your belief system, your mind will cease to assimilate any additional input. You would find yourself in a position where you would need to rectify the other individual's statements, based on your belief that they are inaccurate. Once your mind ceases to process an inflow of information, you relinquish your focus on the subject, interject during the conversation, and delve into a debate about what is correct and incorrect, consequently diverting attention from the main topic of discussion. Validity of one's belief does not necessarily hinge on correctness, as it is shaped by individual experiences that vary amongst individuals.

This will ultimately lead to a compromised relationship.

To circumvent such scenarios, it is advisable to resolve the matter directly with the individual with whom you appear to share a discordant sentiment. By engaging in this action, you will mitigate the risk of harboring any misconceptions or erroneous judgments about the individual in question. Could it be plausible that your acquaintance, who conveys information regarding another individual's remarks about yourself, is endeavoring to portray him in a negative manner? If you persist in exclusively relying on the testimony of your friend, there is a risk of developing a subjective bias.

The optimal approach to safeguard oneself from becoming a target of anger lies in examining and challenging one's erroneous convictions. Once you begin to harbor the belief that the other individual's sole intentions revolve around inflicting emotional or physical harm upon you, it is at this point that you will commence responding in an adverse manner. If left unaddressed, this situation could potentially escalate and result in the deterioration of the friendship or relationship.

Your belief systems yield significant influence in shaping your life, necessitating vigilance in monitoring their impact. Altering your erroneous convictions necessitates engaging in introspective examination. It is crucial to undertake introspection on any event that occurs in your life, which propels you towards the path of anger. If this process of self-reflection is consistently practiced over an extended duration, it will facilitate the implementation of substantial transformations in both your own life and the lives of those you hold dear.

Three: The Imperative of Pursuing Resolutions

In the context of human existence, it is imperative to acknowledge that anger poses a substantive risk and detriment to our physical and psychological welfare. While a justifiable degree of anger can serve as a catalyst for constructive and transformative choices, an excessive amount of anger will invariably inflict physical and psychological harm upon us. Anger undermines our composure and rationality, consequently necessitating the pursuit of remedies to acquire mastery over our emotions. There are numerous justifications for the necessity of seeking solutions once we have acknowledged the presence of anger issues.

1. Anger is associated with a plethora of intricate health complications. Failing to acquire the skill of managing your anger can lead to adverse health outcomes for yourself. One may encounter elevated heart rate, elevated blood pressure, and increased adrenaline levels, leading to the emergence of intensely agitated thoughts. Excessive anger may also contribute to the development of psychiatric disorders and other long-term health conditions.

2. Rage, when left unchecked, undermines and erodes both our interpersonal and professional connections. Our failure to regulate our anger adversely impacts our interpersonal relationships with friends, family members, and colleagues at work. Displaying episodes of anger and

hostility results in the alienation of individuals, ultimately leading to social isolation and the potential demise of one's social connections. Furthermore, it should be noted that anger has the potential to adversely impact one's professional environment. When colleagues refrain from interacting with you during work hours, it undermines the ethos of collaborative effort that is imperative within any professional setting. This results in decreased productivity and may jeopardize one's employment. Despite being the proprietor of the establishment, such a circumstance has the potential to intimidate both clients and employees, possibly resulting in their avoidance.

3. Anger makes us unproductive. Maintaining a sustained state of anger can detrimentally impact productivity, as it convolutes the mind and

compromises one's capacity for rational and cognitive thinking.

4. Anger is spontaneous. The impulsive nature of anger is an additional justification for our pursuit of mastering its regulation. The emotion of anger has the potential to induce uninhibited, impulsive behavior, devoid of conscious awareness or rational understanding. Often, one becomes aware of their actions only once the anger has subsided.

5. Rage is an unambiguous and overt path towards self-annihilation. Uncontrolled anger possesses the capacity to inflict extensive harm across various facets of an individual's life, encompassing emotional well-being, physical health, financial stability, psychological equilibrium, cognitive abilities, educational pursuits, and social relationships.

6. For individuals who are in search of love, anger can pose as an impediment that hinders the ability to establish romantic connections. Due to the perception of being an individual prone to anger and violence, others may choose to distance themselves from you.

These are but a limited selection of the myriad reasons why it is imperative to proactively pursue remedies for our anger before it engulfs and annihilates us. Subsequently, our following will delve into the process of pursuing remedies to anger.

6

Identify and implement innovative strategies to address societal challenges.

The key to addressing the future lies in actively shaping it. —Dennis Gabor

Everyone faces challenges. Challenges are inherent in the human experience, and navigating them is a means by which individuals can cultivate personal development. If it were hypothetically feasible to lead a life devoid of hardships and conflicts, this existence would inevitably result in an impediment to intellectual and emotional growth. However, there are individuals who hold the belief that attaining a state of pure bliss, devoid of any difficulties, is both achievable and desirable. Subsequently, when predicaments arise as anticipated, these individuals become greatly agitated. We perceive the perspective on life held by these individuals as impractical. We strongly uphold the notion that genuine personal growth is attained when an individual can approach challenges with composure, diligently pursue a rational resolution, and subsequently evolve through the course of uncovering such a solution. It is likely that you have observed, though it may be evident that not all individuals acquire greater wisdom as they grow older. Certain individuals experience personal growth as a result of their adversities, while others do not. Individuals who do not possess the capability to let go of their anger are frequently trapped in that emotional state. They express dissatisfaction, endure unhappiness, and frequently encounter social rejection. The consequences arise from your responses to the challenges encountered in your personal journey, irrespective of their magnitude or significance. From one perspective, by perceiving difficulties as opportunities to be conquered and by minimizing feelings of outrage whilst actively addressing these challenges, it is probable that you will achieve gratifying outcomes. Conversely, should you engage in exclaiming loudly, displaying a petulant demeanor, engaging in acts of throwing objects, and refusing to consider alternative viewpoints, it is improbable that you will achieve favorable outcomes.

Developing the ability to respond tactfully to challenging individuals and circumstances necessitates a heightened sense of self-awareness and a willingness to venture into uncharted methods. The manner in which you address challenges greatly influences the trajectory of your life, whether leading to progress, regression, or stagnation. Individuals who cultivate sagacity maintain a composed demeanor, retain knowledge gleaned from prior experiences, and employ said knowledge to discern optimal approaches to forthcoming challenges and gauge their potential outcomes. Throughout our professional endeavors, we have encountered numerous individuals who exhibited a lack of awareness regarding the repercussions of their actions. They endeavored to address issues by fixating on what they perceived as inequitable and unjust treatment inflicted upon them by others.

They voiced their discontent and lamented not only about exceptional hardships but also about commonplace ones. They pondered retribution and indulged in reveries about it. They pouted and shouted. They engaged in a diverse range of detrimental avoidance behaviors, including alcohol consumption, excessive gambling, and substance abuse. They refrained from returning home, attending school, and interacting with family members for extended durations. Evidently, such responses do not result in effective resolution of issues. We regret to inform you that we are unable to provide guidance in addressing the specific challenges you are encountering. You possess the most intimate understanding of your challenges, and you bear the ultimate accountability for the decisions you make. However, within this chapter, we shall endeavor to impart a methodological approach called social problem solving. Through this technique, you will acquire the skills to generate a repertoire of potential solutions for a given problem, carefully select the most optimal solution from this repertoire, and advance your personal development as you navigate your choices.

We believe that there are various options available to you. The manner in which you respond to challenges in the long run will significantly impact the overall quality of your life. In our endeavor to assist you, our utmost aim is to facilitate the attainment of a highly gratifying and optimal life experience. We trust that you will be capable of both mitigating your anger and cultivating more productive resolutions to the difficulties you encounter.

Final Thoughts

At this juncture, I trust that I have successfully elucidated a pivotal aspect: anger arises from one's interpretation of occurrences. Naturally, there are matters that we must unequivocally express our discontent with, notably social injustice. Nevertheless, it is imperative that we pause and thoroughly evaluate the underlying reasons for our emotional distress. It is likely that the aspects that frequently incite anger within you stem from your subjective perception of the surrounding circumstances. Now is the opportune moment for you to reassess your perception of the stimuli that incite your anger.

I am present with the purpose of reminding you that you are not solitary in this endeavor. Similar to yourself, I have experienced this situation, along with numerous other individuals who are parents. Please be mindful that you are not the sole individual in this situation. We all experience it at some point in our lives. Hence, it is imperative for us to allocate sufficient time to discern the most effective strategy for gaining control over our emotions, identifying their triggers, and enhancing our ability to regulate our emotional responses.

In the forthcoming chapters, we shall extensively explore the profound impact that triggers exert on your overall responses to the prevailing circumstances. In particular, we will delve into distinct stimuli and their influence on your reactions to your children's conduct. Please refrain from adjusting the tuning dial, as we have an ample amount of further content in store for your enjoyment.

Formal Operational Stage

At this stage, children have attained proficiency in navigating the environment surrounding them. Children have acquired a comprehensive understanding of key principles pertaining to their immediate environment. They exhibit a high level of autonomy and necessitate minimal oversight in carrying out basic activities such as using the restroom, consuming meals, dressing oneself, and bathing. Children also possess a comparatively strong understanding of their emotions.

Their cognitive abilities enable them to perceive beyond the tangible reality that surrounds them.

Presented below are the notable achievements attained during this particular phase:

Young individuals cultivate the capacity for abstract reasoning within hypothetical scenarios, thereby fostering their ability to enhance problem-solving proficiency.

As children develop, they gradually acquire the capacity to comprehend conceptual ideas related to morality, ethics, societal matters, and even political issues.

Children employ deductive reasoning in order to surpass broad generalizations and delve into more specific information and data.

During the transition to adolescence, the rate of physical development in children may exceed their emotional and cognitive maturation. Hence, it is incumbent upon parents to provide children with the necessary reassurance to navigate through the most perplexing phases of their lives.

As is evident, Piaget was indeed onto something. His contributions laid the groundwork for our contemporary comprehension of the development of children. Nevertheless, it is evident that his work was predominantly unfinished. The notion that development essentially concludes at the age of 12 appears to lack foresight. It has been determined that the development of children extends significantly throughout their adolescent years. Consequently, contemporary psychologists have taken Piaget's innovative research and adapted it to align with our present comprehension of the growth and development of children.

4

Types of anger

There are a variety of anger disorders that individuals often encounter when faced with challenges in effectively controlling their anger. Numerous authorities in the field of psychology have disseminated a diverse array of anger disorders, which often exhibit substantial inconsistencies with one another. Nevertheless, in this context, I will solely address the prevalent manifestations of anger to prevent any potential inconsistencies.

Passive anger

Individuals of this kind often remain unaware of their own anger. When one experiences latent anger, the displayed emotions often manifest as sarcasm, cruelty, or even apathy. In the majority of instances, individuals exhibiting such tendencies have been observed to partake in specific conduct, including absenteeism from work or school, as well as social withdrawal. They likewise exhibit subpar performance, particularly when engaging in social and professional gatherings. Individuals may perceive your behavior as self-sabotage, even in the absence of your awareness and ability to justify your actions.

On certain occasions, anger may be suppressed, rendering it considerably challenging to perceive. Given such circumstances, the sole course of action that holds potential is to discern the underlying sentiment fueling your behaviors, enabling you to effectively unearth the source provoking your ire and thereby address it accordingly.

Aggressive anger

Individuals who encounter this specific form of anger typically possess mindfulness concerning their emotional state, albeit they may not invariably comprehend the underlying source of their aggressive behavior. In alternative scenarios, it is not uncommon to observe individuals transferring their aggressive outbursts towards scapegoats. This presents a significant difficulty when it comes to addressing the underlying issue. It is important to highlight that violent outbursts or acts of revenge are characteristic of the manifestation of aggressive anger. It has the potential to inflict physical harm upon individuals or cause damage to their personal belongings. Hence, it is imperative to acquire the aptitude to identify catalysts of anger in order to proficiently manage manifestations when they manifest and approach them in a more constructive and positive manner.

Assertive anger

This form of anger represents a prominent illustration of individuals utilizing their aggression to enact beneficial transformations. Nevertheless, this implies that rather than evading conflicts or internalizing anger, you opt to articulate it in a manner that induces transformative outcomes while avoiding harm or distress.

Assertive anger is predominantly perceived as a potent catalyst that empowers individuals to realize their aspirations in life.

Behavioral anger

For this category, there is a frequent manifestation of physical violence. Individuals who exhibit this form of anger frequently experience a sense of emotional inundation, leading them to express their rage by lashing out at objects. "It typically engenders considerable unpredictability and significantly alters the trajectory of their lives, primarily stemming from legal and interpersonal ramifications."

Given the intensity of this anger, it is imperative to pause and collect oneself before engaging in actions that could have enduring consequences. This can be achieved by disengaging from the situation and employing introspective self-dialogue to regain command.

2. Inaccurate interpretation of nonverbal cues and verbal communication

Regardless of its apparent simplicity, we all fall prey to this phenomenon. What eludes our comprehension is this fundamental truth - our nonverbal cues communicate before we are afforded an opportunity to vocalize. I consistently remind my adolescent daughter that her demeanor precedes her communication, and therefore she must be conscious of how she presents herself.

Please exercise caution regarding the nonverbal cues displayed by your body. One's body communicates through various nonverbal cues such as facial expressions, the position of their shoulders, their posture, and their overall stance. It is important to bear in mind that all individuals are interconnected, thus this should be taken into consideration while engaging in communication with others.

Furthermore, apart from nonverbal cues, verbal communication is also present. Each individual's comprehension inevitably relies on their unique perspective and interpretation, as it is frequently remarked that misinterpretations can occur during the process of translation. It is a humorous yet accurate observation.

It is important to bear in mind that each person possesses a personal history replete with various life encounters, and that certain words can have a detrimental impact, based on subjective interpretation. Please bear in mind that this constitutes a crucial aspect of communication.

3. Lack of information

Indeed, individuals tend to respond in accordance with the knowledge they possess. Please ensure that you provide sufficient details to facilitate the resolution of any potential misconceptions. It is advisable to refrain from treating anything, or anyone in particular, as a given.

One additional humorous idiom that is familiar to us all is as follows: 'One should avoid making assumptions, as doing so may lead to one appearing foolish in the presence of others.' I have deep appreciation for it as it effectively facilitates the process of analyzing and reflecting upon matters, and it is crucial for us to engage in such behavior before responding.

Presented herewith are several indicators that individuals in a committed partnership ought to duly acknowledge within the context of their relationship.

Exhibiting mindfulness of one's emotional state.

It is essential for both individuals involved in a relationship to possess the capability to recognize and regulate their emotions for the purpose of successfully resolving any issues that may arise. Once there is introspection and self-awareness regarding one's identity and emotions, the subsequent choice of reaction will significantly shape one's impact on others.

Displaying a confident and self-assured demeanor in one's communication with others.

Self-expression is an essential component within the context of every interpersonal relationship. Everyone should feel comfortable to freely express themselves under any circumstances. Ultimately, this is an integral facet of fostering and nurturing relationships. The introductory phase of acquainting oneself.

It is possible for an individual to appear assertive or potentially aggressive, though their intention may actually be to protect their emotions in some manner. This should be explicit in all relationships. Furthermore, communication holds immense importance for another reason.

Discussing not only positive emotions but also unfavorable ones.

Equally significant is the manner in which the sentiment is conveyed. This can also serve as a catalyst for occasionally eliciting undesirable emotions. An additional commonly used expression is, 'The manner in which something is conveyed carries greater significance than the content itself.' It is important to exercise caution and consideration in communication.

Expectations From Birth To The Third Year

From the moment of a child's birth until their twelfth month, one of the most formidable challenges for parents lies in the emotionally and physically draining nature of handling tantrums. It is customary to experience frustration when one's infant grasps onto their nose and refuses to release it, removes their earrings, tugs on their hair, or bites while breastfeeding. Contrarily, infants exhibit no deliberate inclination to inflict harm or anguish upon those whom they hold dear. They are employing their sensory capabilities to explore their environment. Children acquire an understanding of the functioning of the world through the processes of biting, orally exploring objects, grasping, shaking and releasing, swatting, and subsequently observing the ensuing consequences, often resulting in a notable reaction.

During the period spanning from the twelfth month to the twenty-fourth month, tantrums such as hitting, kicking, biting, among other behaviors, tend to reach their maximum intensity. This is primarily due to the fact that toddlers at this stage experience heightened emotions that they are unable to express adequately through verbal communication. Young children are also deficient in the capability to exhibit self-restraint when it comes to refraining from acting on their emotions. They are merely in the early stages of cultivating empathy or acquiring the capacity to comprehend the emotional states of others. However, they are unable to express their feelings as, "Mother, I am displeased due to the fact that Jeff took possession of my cherished doll." "Nevertheless, I am aware that his intentions are simply to engage in enjoyable playtime with me." Considering the child's propensity for using a toy truck to strike Jeff, perhaps it would be more prudent to explore alternative options rather than obtaining a new doll for his amusement.

Between the twenty-fourth and thirty-sixth month of a child's development, it is common for toddlers to exhibit aggressive behaviors, such as physically lashing out at a parent, in response to distressing situations or intense emotions like anger or jealousy. These instances can be particularly challenging for parents due to the emotional distress they cause. Parents frequently assume that as their young children develop their cognitive abilities and enhance their linguistic capabilities, they will inevitably demonstrate an increased level of self-regulation. This developmental stage can be puzzling due to the fact that, although a two-and-a-half-year-old may understand the rule, they may struggle with inhibiting their impulses to engage in desired behaviors. In the present age, the dominance of emotions often supersedes the faculties of reason.

In essence, it can be concluded that when a young child displays anger, it signifies a loss of command over their emotions, necessitating the restoration of composure prior to engaging in any form of instruction or acquisition of knowledge. Maintaining composure is the optimal course of action, as it enables your child to mirror your composed demeanor.

Personify their rage

The presence of our anger is inherent within us, yet it need not exert dominion over our actions. Fury is a potent sentiment that can appear intimidating and perturbing to young individuals. Incorporating the practice of transferring a child's problem or challenge onto an external entity is a highly effective therapeutic approach that I frequently employ when working with children. If your child encounters challenges in effectively handling their anger, assigning a designated name and visual representation to their anger facilitates the process of distinguishing their underlying identity from the problematic anger manifestations. It is imperative to recognize that the individual's essence is not inherently faulty, rather it is the anger-related impediments that must be addressed. When a child perceives themselves as being troubled due to their frequent disruptive behavior in school or the creation of disturbances at home, the task of facilitating their progress becomes increasingly arduous.

Provide a concise statement to your child, such as, "It appears that feelings of intense anger have been considerably burdening you recently." "Why don't we assign a name to your anger and create a visual representation of how you imagine it might appear?" By enabling the child to perceive the issue from an external perspective, they can engage in rational problem-solving and gain heightened understanding of the problem or situation at hand.

The Surface Manifestations of Anger

Anger is a multifaceted emotional state, and the greater comprehension your child possesses regarding its mechanisms, the more proficient they will become in managing it. Anger is occasionally employed as a defense mechanism or a façade to conceal underlying empathetic sentiments.

It is more effortless to succumb to anger rather than experience the emotions of humiliation, embarrassment, or pain. The subconscious mind is inclined to safeguard our well-being, thus deploying its defensive mechanisms. The anger iceberg metaphor serves as an excellent visual representation that effectively illustrates this concept to children while also fostering their self-awareness. Each day, children experience a range of activities, emotions, and stressors that remain hidden beneath the surface, out of view from parents or teachers. By encouraging children to reflect on their various emotions and circumstances throughout the day or week, they can then record these beneath the surface of their anger iceberg. Through this process, when a child directs their attention towards their authentic emotions and stressors, you are able to assist them in effectively navigating and resolving complex emotional challenges.

WHAT'S YOUR STYLE?

W

hat's your parenting style?

Does that inquiry bear resemblance? When were you initially introduced to the concept of "parenting style?" Was it through an online questionnaire? A magazine?On the parents\\\' forum?

Irrespective of the source from which you obtained this information, it is highly probable that you did not accord it significant attention. And that is acceptable, considering the fact that you were not provided with a comprehensive guide on successful parenting upon the arrival of your child.

Despite being widely used, there remains a lack of comprehension among individuals regarding the substantial influence that our parenting approach has on our children. It exerts an influence on their character, physical well-being, emotional well-being, and psychological well-being. Hence, acquiring proficiency in your chosen parenting approach and seeking avenues to enhance its efficacy not only positions you as an exceptional caregiver but also establishes the trajectory for your child's accomplishment in life.

Fortunately, the consequences of specific parental approaches are not uniformly unidirectional. Nevertheless, it is crucial to comprehend diverse parenting approaches and their potential effects on a child's growth and maturation.

Given the substantial disparity in our individual conceptions of an exceptional parent, it is advisable for you to acquire attributes from the particular approaches you deem instrumental in manifesting your desired parenthood.

PARENTING STYLES

A parenting style can be defined as the manner in which parents engage in their interactions with their children. This interaction is indicative of the parents' values, beliefs, and their own background as recipients of parenting. In assessing an individual's parenting style, numerous factors are taken into account, encompassing, yet not restricted to:

Does the parent exhibit acts of selflessness and make personal sacrifices for the child's benefit?

How kindly and compassionate is the parent's demeanor towards the child?

What are the parent's expectations regarding the child's level of responsibility?

To what extent does the parent attend to the child's needs (promptly or negligently)?

Does the parent employ assertive communication techniques or exhibit a calm and patient demeanor when engaging with others in the household?

The degree of self-discipline demonstrated by the parent.

These can be classified into three distinct categories: the manner in which parents demonstrate affection towards their offspring, how parents manage their children's wants and necessities, and the approach parents adopt to enforce their parental control.

Nevertheless, it is unequivocal that the manner in which a parent communicates is greatly shaped by the environment in which they were brought up. In the 1960s, Diana Baumrind initially proposed the categorization of parents into four distinct groups upon introducing the concept.

Authoritative parenting

Authoritarian parenting

Permissive parenting

Uninvolved/neglectful parenting

Upon conducting in-depth research on the science of family socialization, scholars have identified three additional categories:

Free-range parenting

Helicopter parenting

Attachment parenting

In the subsequent section, we will extensively explore the intricacies of each parenting style, provide illustrative instances of said styles, and delineate the advantages and disadvantages associated with each approach.

Come along.

3. Unequal treatment

On which occasion did you most recently find yourself drawing comparisons between the manner in which you were treated and the treatment received by others in your professional environment? At some point or another, the majority of individuals have contemplated inquiries such as: "For what reason was she awarded a bonus while I was not?" I exert the same level of effort in my work," "He was not meritorious of that promotion," "I have recently successfully concluded a significant project within the allocated timeframe and budget, yet my achievements were not acknowledged to the same extent as his," or "I am curious if his salary surpasses mine.

It is inherent for individuals to engage in self-comparisons with others within the professional environment. Frequently, this comparison is predicated on a "reciprocal exchange" ratio. You possess qualities such as diligent effort, academic pursuit, or innate aptitude. By fulfilling these responsibilities, you will receive remuneration, career advancement opportunities, and acknowledgment. However, upon uncovering disparities in the distribution of resources relative to others, it is plausible to experience a sense of frustration, particularly in instances where a colleague is contributing less yet reaping greater benefits. Disparities in treatment represent an additional prevalent source of workplace dissatisfaction.

Question

Frances is frustrated due to the fact that Niles consistently has the privilege of selecting his shifts ahead of her, leaving her perplexed about the reasoning behind it. Based on their performance, representatives are afforded the privilege of selecting their shifts in priority.

Fran is situated alongside Niles and is aware of his frequent tardiness for shifts and when resuming work after breaks, whereas Fran consistently arrives punctually for work and rarely exceeds the allocated time for her breaks. Niles has provided his call quality scores, thereby confirming that she also possesses superior call quality. However, he consistently has the privilege of selecting his shifts ahead of her.

Do you believe Fran is expressing anger as a result of being subjected to unjust treatment?

Options:

1. Yes

2. No

Answer

Fran is displeased due to her perception that Niles is receiving a greater share without adequately contributing, thereby causing a sense of dissatisfaction. The likelihood of arousing feelings of anger is highly probable when individuals perceive disparities in treatment.

Based on the preceding situation, Fran was able to ascertain the presence of unequal treatment due to the fact that the conditions for being eligible for shift premium were explicitly established and conveyed to all personnel. Nevertheless, it is prudent to bear in mind that typically, these juxtapositions derive from your perspective rather than objective reality. Occasionally, it can be your perception that is inaccurate rather than the treatment itself.

Quinton's tenure with his current employer spans a duration of merely six months. The organization is consistently engaging in the hiring process for sales positions. He holds the belief that the newly recruited employees are being presented with more attractive incentives, including upgraded workstations, enhanced compensation packages, and a higher initial salary, in comparison to the incentives that were offered to him during his own recruitment, thus resulting in his current state of anger.

It is imperative to acknowledge that irrespective of Quinton's perception of unfair treatment or the actual occurrence of unequal treatment, it can give rise to feelings of anger stemming from the disparity in treatment.

Rejection

One significant cause of frustration that manifests both in our personal lives and within the professional setting revolves around the experience of being rejected. When experiencing invalidation, there is a notable erosion of one's sense of inherent worth and respect. In the majority of instances, the individual or collective entity in question is not deliberately endeavoring to induce within us a sensation of being excluded. However, we might perceive their actions as deliberate, thereby causing us emotional distress.

Examples of rejection:

In the event that an individual imparts the impression that your contributions in both domestic and professional spheres fall short, despite your evident dedication and competence, it is likely to induce feelings of exclusion, fostering a sense of inadequacy and resentment within you.

In instances where your company bestows accolades or advancements upon individuals who contribute equivalently or perhaps even less than you do, there arises a sense of inequitable treatment. One starts to develop a perception that their company fails to acknowledge the value of their contributions and disregards their worth as a valuable resource, leading to feelings of rejection and resentment.

When subjected to derogatory and dismissive communication from one's superior, partner, or guardian, with little regard for one's perspective, guidance, or emotions, one experiences a sense of being marginalized and incurs feelings of resentment.

These sentiments of insufficiency, exclusion, and nullification are pervasive. You sense a distinct undermining of your value, competence, and intellectual capacity, resulting in considerable distress. When an individual dismisses our needs, it engenders internal upheaval.

It is imperative that we select self-validation as our guiding principle, refusing to allow external parties to determine our worth. When it seems that others fail to recognize your value, it is important to tackle the matter in a genuine and constructive manner, refraining from any detrimental emotional outbursts. Moreover, although you may perceive your feelings of rejection or unmet needs as valid, it is crucial to consider the potential for misdirected anger. The source of misguided anger originates from self-centered desires and excessive or shallow needs, or from an unrealistic expectation of perfection in others, a standard that is arduous for any individual to attain.

Taking these factors into consideration, it is plausible that you may have already identified the cause of your anger. However, it is highly probable that the root of this anger lies deeply ingrained within you, posing a challenge to unveil. The generation of fury does not arise from an individual or a particular occurrence. Though specific individuals and specific undertakings may provoke a reaction, anger is a considerably intricate emotion that necessitates introspective exploration to uncover its origins.

In order to provide you with a more comprehensive understanding of potential triggers, we shall examine alternative factors that contribute to feelings of anger and fury.

Acquire Awareness Of Your Triggers And Employ Efficient Strategies For Their Management

Anyone has the ability to experience anger - a relatively straightforward task. However, to direct one's anger towards the appropriate individual, at the precise intensity and moment, for a valid motive, and in a suitable manner - this is not a capability possessed by everyone, nor is it a simple undertaking.

Aristotle

Lack of awareness regarding the causes or triggers behind one's anger can perpetuate the issue and exacerbate its severity over time.

Once you are prepared to undertake the endeavor, enhance your cognizance of the stimuli that provoke you, thus enabling you to discern what causes agitation and intensifies your indignation. It is necessary to explore alternative coping mechanisms that will aid in effectively managing your anger.

Beforehand, it is imperative that you prepare yourself through training to perceive the subtle and overt indications of anger, thus enabling you to detect the gradual emergence of this emotion.

Acquire the skill of identifying and discerning your emotions of anger.

It is imperative that one possesses the ability to promptly discern the nascent manifestations of anger within oneself, enabling the opportunity to undertake proper measures to address and manage these incipient stages of anger before they escalate into a state of complete fury.

The preceding elucidated the indicators and manifestations of anger, along with furnishing you with a convenient methodology for monitoring these indicators. As you cultivate an increased awareness of your emotions and articulate your anger, it is paramount to remain mindful of these indicators.

If you tend to experience the onset of anger as a sensation of discomfort in your abdominal region, which then intensifies as you dwell on distressing thoughts or situations, or engage in restless pacing due to extreme agitation, make a conscious effort to increase your awareness of that initial sense of uneasiness. Once you become aware of this, you must recognize that an eruption of anger is imminent and must be addressed before reaching the stage of manifesting it.

Begin cultivating a heightened sense of mindfulness towards your physical and mental state by allocating approximately 2 to 5 minutes of solitary contemplation to oneself, at minimum 3 to 5 occasions daily. A duration of five minutes may appear brief, nonetheless, if one assumes a state of tranquil introspection and attentively observes the influx, flow, and subsequent departure of sensations, cognitions, and sentiments within oneself, a substantial understanding of one's corporeal existence may be gained.

Contemplate your emotional state, contemplate the thoughts that arise and dissipate within your consciousness, and consider their impact on your overall disposition. If you detect a slight indication of anger manifesting in your body or conduct, endeavor to maintain composure and simply engage in mindful observation of it. What implications can be drawn about your mood from this? This brief, 5-minute exercise in mindful observation of one's thoughts and emotions, particularly anger, facilitates enhanced understanding of personal emotions, thereby facilitating the ability to readily discern what provokes them.

Identify the factors that provoke your frustration

Retrieve the documentation of your anger indicators and utilize it to develop a more comprehensive comprehension of the stimuli that provoke your anger. As your awareness of your emotions and the associated signs of anger, both emotional, physical, and behavioral, increases, you will acquire the ability to utilize them in order to identify the underlying cause.

A trigger can encompass anything that elicits or incites feelings of anger within an individual. It could involve engaging in conversation with another individual, reminiscent contemplation, encountering circumstances such as a congested traffic flow, executing tasks unsuccessfully, and so forth. Whenever you perceive the emergence of anger within your emotional realm, diligently observe it in a composed manner whilst reflecting upon the thought, encounter, circumstance, or individual responsible for its arousal.

As an illustration, if one were to raise their voice at their child, was it prompted by genuine anger towards the child, or did it stem from an alternative source? It is possible that you and your spouse recently engaged in a heated disagreement, causing you to redirect your frustration towards your child instead of exacerbating the situation by venting it on your partner.

Engage in a more profound exploration of the factors that trigger your anger in order to gain a comprehensive understanding of its underlying causes.

It is crucial to emphasize the fundamental factors contributing to the manifestation of anger.

Occasionally, the intensity of your anger surpasses apparent observations. While it might appear that your anger stems from the traffic jam, it is conceivable that it is instead rooted in your inability to relinquish the memory of your friend's betrayal. One may exhibit persistent episodes of anger while neglecting to acknowledge that such anger stems from enduring stress caused by issues in interpersonal connections and vocational challenges. While engaging in the process of analyzing the fundamental origins and stimuli of one's anger, it is imperative to meticulously observe the underlying rationales and intricacies.

It is advisable to meticulously document all your discoveries to maintain a comprehensive record and utilize them in formulating suitable strategies to address your predicament.

3: Familiarize Yourself With Your Anger Patterns

Although it is accurate to state that individuals will inevitably have varying experiences with anger, it must be noted that there exists a significant extent of commonality among them, potentially surpassing one's initial perceptions. In a general sense, anger can be classified according to five distinct manifestations:

The intended goal of the anger (whether punitive or restorative) is to be pursued.

The extent to which anger induces impulsiveness (unrestrained or regulated).

The overarching manifestation of ire (expressed through speech or action)

The response elicited by anger (marked by resistance or retaliation)

The orientation of anger (outward or inward)

Furthermore, it is imperative to bear in mind that your displeasure may manifest itself predominantly in various manners contingent upon the circumstances, whether it be a sense of frustration or a perception of being disregarded or endangered. One should bear in mind that anger itself possesses neither inherent goodness nor badness; its negative connotation arises from the manner in which certain individuals choose to manifest their anger. Therefore, it is imperative to establish the specific nature of your anger as an initial measure in managing the outward manifestation of your emotions and consequently moderating your responsive behaviors.

Assertive anger

Amongst the various forms of anger, assertive anger proves to be the most advantageous in terms of its productivity. This particular form of anger frequently manifests through the utilization of intense feelings of fury or exasperation as catalysts for constructive transformation. Rather than evading conflict or displaying physical or emotional volatility, this form of anger typically motivates individuals to take action and personally address the root cause that triggered their anger.

This category of anger frequently serves as a potent catalyst, capable of surmounting an array of alternative emotions, such as intense fear. The primary obstacle associated with this form of anger lies in effectively channeling it and fully leveraging its power as a source of motivation, prior to its dissipation and subsequent acceptance of the existing situation.

Behavioral anger

This form of anger is predominantly communicated through physical actions, and the manifestations of these actions can be highly aggressive. Individuals who encounter this particular form of anger frequently encounter a sense of being overcome by their emotions, which results in their tendency to display uncontrolled behavior towards the source of their anger. If allowed to go unaddressed, such anger can precipitate instances of physical altercation and frequently result in adverse and uncertain ramifications on both interpersonal relationships and legal matters.

When addressing the management of this form of anger, the most effective course of action in the present moment would be to grant oneself a degree of distance from the subject matter provoking one's agitation. This will afford you the chance to restore your mental equilibrium and employ any of the strategies elucidated in the subsequent chapters, thereby averting actions that are highly probable to evoke regret. While there exist a myriad of enduring solutions one can diligently pursue to prevent the escalation of anger towards such violent thresholds, this uncomplicated and efficacious alternative can safeguard you against an array of regrettable actions you would prefer to avoid. Once you have regained composure, you will probably discover that it is possible to reassess the situation from an entirely alternative perspective.

4: Examine the Four Phases of Anger

Have you ever taken a moment to ponder the process of experiencing anger? Undoubtedly, it is indeed a process. I understand that it may appear that you transition swiftly from a calm state to a state of intense rage. However, upon closer examination of the circumstances, if you engage in introspection and evaluate your actions and emotions, you will realize that becoming genuinely angry is a process that requires a certain amount of time. The ire manifests as your emotions escalate.

Allow me to provide an illustrative instance – I formerly struggled with issues pertaining to anger, as I have previously alluded to on multiple occasions. Instant provocation was not the source of my reaction; instead, it was a gradual yet undeniable accumulation over time. It commences with minor and vexing inconveniences, gradually escalating as your dissatisfaction intensifies, eventually leading to an explosive outburst or impulsive act of aggression towards an unsuspecting piece of furniture. Please exercise caution, as you run the risk of causing harm to yourself.

By devoting one's time to observing another individual, or even intentionally seeking to incite their anger in a malevolent manner, one can witness the various stages that an individual undergoes as they progress toward the zenith of their anger. From a sociological perspective, it can be intriguing, albeit perilous, if one fails to seek shelter.

Stage 1: Annoyance

The manner in which it is evident: The experience of feeling irritated is fundamentally ingrained in our everyday lives. There exists a multitude of inconsequential matters that have the potential to incite annoyance within us, with varying degrees of intensity. Nonetheless, these inconveniences are trivial and pose no significant disruption to our daily routines. Slightly invasive and eliciting slight irritation, nuisances arise consistently throughout the process and cannot be circumvented. Hence, they do not justify expending energy and becoming agitated due to them.

Given that this is solely the initial phase and lacks any substantial implications, the duration of the anger is not protracted. It fleetingly materializes and dematerializes without leaving a lasting impact. Given that it has minimal impact on your well-being, you are able to maintain composure and logically deduce that this situation is not of significant consequence. Displeasure does not elicit any discernible alteration in behavior. Once you return to the comfort of your abode after a long day of toiling, the exasperation caused by the malfunctioning of your computer mouse earlier shall dissipate from your memory.

What causes displeasure: In a broad sense, anything has the potential to be a source of annoyance for individuals. From the manner in which an individual consumes their food to the selection of music broadcasted on the radio, to even the persistent presence of an irksome mosquito depriving one of rest, inconveniences of a trivial nature are undeniably abundant and varied. Some may argue that these annoyances contribute to the intriguing aspects of life, although perhaps that may not be universally agreed upon. However, they should not elicit excessive agitation.

Frequent inconveniences comprise individuals who disregard proper queue etiquette, the regrettable instance of discovering that your feline companion has defecated on the carpet, as well as the undesirable behavior of your cohabitant in leaving their soiled hosiery strewn across the floor, among other examples.

Stage 2: Frustration

How it presents itself: Frustration is also a prevalent manifestation, but unlike annoyance, which typically arises from immediate factors, frustration stems from persistent irritating actions. One becomes exasperated when confronted with the repetitive occurrence of a trivial matter. At this juncture, your patience is progressively dwindling, and although you maintain a calm and composed demeanor, beneath this facade, your frustration is quietly simmering. It's just so frustrating!

Although prevalent feelings of frustration persist within the realm of reason, there is a genuine risk that they may gradually dissipate. The tiniest catalyst can swiftly propel you into the subsequent phase of anger, yet presently, you find yourself regrettably trapped in the state of frustration, compelled to endure the persistent vexation until it becomes overwhelming. Alternatively, one could contemplate the termination of the source of their vexation.

www.ingramcontent.com/pod-product-compliance
Lightning Source LLC
Chambersburg PA
CBHW052136110526
44591CB00012B/1751